I LIVE WITH AUTISM

WRITTEN BY CHRISTINA EARLEY

ILLUSTRATED BY
AMANDA HUDSON

A Starfish Book

SEAHORSE
PUBLISHING

Teaching Tips for Caregivers:

As a caregiver, you can help your child succeed in school by giving them a strong foundation in language and literacy skills and a desire to learn to read.

This book helps children grow by letting them practice reading skills.

Reading for pleasure and interest will help your child to develop reading skills and will give your child the opportunity to practice these skills in meaningful ways.

- Encourage your child to read on her own at home
- Encourage your child to practice reading aloud
- Encourage activities that require reading
- Establish a reading time
- Talk with your child
- Give your child writing materials

Teaching Tips for Teachers:

Research shows that one of the best ways for students to learn a new topic is to read about it.

Before Reading

- Read the "Words to Know" and discuss the meaning of each word.
- Read the back cover to see what the book is about.

During Reading

- When a student gets to a word that is unknown, ask them to look at the rest of the sentence to find clues to help with the meaning of the unknown word.
- Ask the student to write down any pages of the book that were confusing to them.

After Reading

- Discuss the main idea of the book.
- Ask students to give one detail that they learned in the book by showing a text dependent answer from the book.

TABLE OF CONTENTS

I Live with Autism

Hi! My name is Summer.

I am nine years old.

I live with my mom, dad, older brother, and younger sister. Cookie is my bearded dragon.

I was born with autism and am **neurodivergent**.

I do not like to be hugged.

I get **anxious** when I **interact** with others.
I practice what I am going to say.

Autism is a **development** and brain **disorder**.

It affects how people communicate, learn, and behave.

I ride the bus to school. I sit with my friend Kym.

I tell her all about reptiles.
I am an expert!

🕐	MON	TUE	WED	THU	FRI
9am	📖	🖌️	📖	+ − × =	🏀
10am	📖	🖌️	🎵	+ − × =	🏀
12pm	🍎	🍎	🍎	🍎	🍎
1pm	+ − × =	📓	💻	🎵	📓
2pm	+ − × =	🏀	💻	🖌️	📓

I have a schedule with pictures on my desk. I like to know what is coming next.

Miss April helps me with my classwork.
She explains things to me again.

I always eat crunchy carrots and crispy pretzels for lunch.

I wear headphones because the cafeteria is very loud.

My art teacher Mrs. Sakura sometimes lets me draw cartoons.

I would like to be an **animator** when I grow up. What would you like to be?

LEARN ABOUT AUTISM

What Is Autism?

Autism is a brain disorder that causes people to have restricted interests, repetitive behaviors, and difficulty with social communication and interaction. Not all people with autism will have all these. Autistic people use the word *neurodiverse* to explain the differences, abilities, and strengths of their brains.

Difficulty with social communication and interaction is common. Some autistic people do not seem to look at or listen to others who are talking. Others might talk about a particular topic, but not realize the other person is not interested. People with autism might have rigid routines.

Some are sensitive to temperature, texture, smell, or sound. Having strong specific interests is common.

People with autism also have strengths. Many excel in technical and logical subjects like science, engineering, and math. Being precise and detail-oriented is beneficial. Having a unique perspective allows for creative problem-solving.

Although autism is a lifelong condition, children and adults who are provided with the right supports can lead fulfilling lives in school, at work, in relationships, and in their communities.

Websites to Visit

Autism Highway: autismhwy.com

Autism Science Foundation: autismsciencefoundation.org

Autistic Inclusive Meets: autisticinclusivemeets.org

Autistic Self Advocacy Network: autisticadvocacy.org

Organization for Autism Research: researchautism.org

Take the Pledge for Inclusion

☑   I accept people of all abilities.

☑   I respect others and act with kindness and compassion.

☑   I include people with special needs and disabilities in my school and in my community.

Get your parent's permission to sign the online pledge at PledgeforInclusion.org.

Famous People with Autism

Lewis Carroll: Author of *Alice's Adventures in Wonderland*

Albert Einstein: Scientist and mathematician

Temple Grandin: Scientist

Lionel Messi: Professional soccer player

Satoshi Tajiri: Creator of Pokémon

Greta Thunberg: Environmental activist

Lionel Messi

Greta Thunberg

Celebrate and Educate

Neurodiversity Celebration Month happens in April.

World Autism Month happens in April.

World Autism Awareness Day is April 2nd.

Inclusive Schools Week is the first full week in December.

WORDS TO KNOW

animator (an-uh-MAY-tur): a person who draws cartoons that move

anxious (ANGK-shuhs): feeling nervous, worried, or fearful

development (di-VEL-uhp-muhnt): process of growing

disorder (dis-OR-dur): a physical or mental condition that is unusual

interact (in-tur-AKT): to respond to others and talk to them in a social situation

neurodivergent (nur-oh-dye-VER-juhnt): having a brain that works differently

INDEX

COMPREHENSION QUESTIONS

1. Summer has a pet ___.

    a. snake

    b. fish

    c. bearded dragon

2. For lunch, Summer always eats foods that are ___.

    a. soft

    b. crunchy

    c. cold

3. Autism is a disorder of the ___.

    a. muscles

    b. brain

    c. skeleton

4. True or False: Summer likes to be hugged.

5. True or False: Summer likes to draw cartoons.

Answers: 1. c, 2. b, 3. b, 4. False, 5. True

ABOUT THE AUTHOR

Christina Earley lives in sunny south Florida with her son, husband, and rescue dog. She has been teaching children with special needs for over 25 years. She loves to bake cookies, read books about animals, and ride roller coasters.

Written by: Christina Earley
Illustrated by: Amanda Hudson
Design by: Under the Oaks Media
Editor: Kim Thompson

Photos: A.Taoualit/Shutterstock: p. 21 (Lionel Messi); Antonello Marangi/Shutterstock: p. 21 (Greta Thunberg)

Library of Congress PCN Data
I Live with Autism /Christina Earley
I Live With
ISBN 979-8-8873-5344-9(hard cover)
ISBN 979-8-8873-5429-3(paperback)
ISBN 979-8-8873-5514-6(EPUB)
ISBN 979-8-8873-5599-3(eBook)
Library of Congress Control Number: 2022948914

Printed in the United States of America.

Seahorse Publishing Company

www.seahorsepub.com

Published in the United States
Seahorse Publishing
PO Box 771325
Coral Springs, FL 33077